I CHOOSE TO BE INDEPENDENT

THE WOUNDS OF PAST, FREEDOM OF TODAY!

RUCHI KARKI

ISBN 979-888606448-3

Contents

Preface

Did you ever wonder how India's Independence has been possible?

How freedom fighters struggled?

Question that should be in the mind of every Indian.

I have seen people around me who are enjoying their freedom, but still did not know the struggle behind that freedom.

In this book I will explore the struggle behind Indian Independence and new perspective related to political cultural economic or science related aspects of National Movement.

A Note From Author

It gives me great pleasure to greet all the people of India living in the country and abroad. My book I choose to be independent fills with the advent of knowing how we struggled earlier, "The wounds of past and freedom of today ".

Also the youth of India should be the special pride of being citizen of a free Nation. We gratefully remember of freedom fighters and Martyrs Who sacrifices have enabled us to live in an independent nation. The ethos of our freedom struggle forms the foundation of modern India.

Lead leaders bought together a diversity of world views to forge a common national spirit. They were committed to the cause of liberating Bharat Mata from opressive foreign rule and secure the future of her children. Their thoughts and actions shaped the identity of India as a modern nation.

We are fortunate that our freedom fighters become the guiding light o We are fortunate that our freedom fighters become the guiding light off of our freedom movement. We have a lot to offer the global community especially for intellectual and spiritual Enrichment and promotion world peace with respect of prayer for developing of one and all :-

सर्वे भवंतु सुखिन :, सर्वे संतु निरामया : ,
सर्वे भद्राणि पश्यंतु, मा कश्चित् दु:खभाग भवेत् ।।

It means may all be happy may all be free from illness All see what is auspicious mein no one comes to grief this message of prayer for Universal well-being iof prayer for Universal wellbeing in india. It is unique gift of humanity.

Jai Hind !

To be continued.........

CHAPTER ONE

RELATIONSHIP ESTABLISHMENT

Freedom the part of everyone's life. The life of an Independent is not only freedom. From our childhood, we want freedom we want to walk ourselves, want to speak our own words and even as we grow our freedom rise, it's demand we want our own rules in our life. Freedom for life has a different meaning but when it comes to the nation than it becomes everything. Freedom of the nation means to create a nation that gives the right to do everything freely in the nation. There are many nations who fought for their freedom, India one of the nation that creates history in struggling for freedom.

India a vast country and has a huge army but then also it has been ruled by different persons and nations. People have to fight for their freedom. The legal rights were not given to the people of the nation. The British ruled India for nearly 200 years and exploited the peoples of India although having numerous army At that time, the question arose, how to start for the independence of the country. India was not able to get the freedom until the peoples get united and fought in an organization. There are numerous organization and army troops formed let's read about these in brief and also check the conclusion of the Indian freedom struggle.

British in India

British has started to conquer India during the Battle of Plassey in 1757. The Beitishehsr's achieve political power in India. The establishment of political power and the company was during the time period of lord governor Dalhousie. During the tenure of Lord Dalhousie, the company almost started to rule entire India. In 1948 Lord Dalhousie Became the governor-general of India. This was the best time of the British in India.

First Revolution of India

The very first revolution for freedom was started in 1847. The revolution was started but the unity causes and becomes the failure of the struggle. The main lead was done by the Rani Laxmi Bai the queen of Jhansi. This can be the victory for the nation but the conclusion of the struggle for the nation was only the start. The seed of freedom and feeling of nationalism was uprooted in India.

Revolt of 1857

After the end of the time period of the governor Lord Dalhousie. The Indians again formed a new revolution this revolution was almost all around the nation. The new thing about this revolution is it was started by the solider's who are in the army of British. The Hindu and Muslim both were equally joined the revolution in the nation. This there was unity but the timing of the revolution was not perfect which causes failure. Thus the struggle for freedom was not over the seed of freedom has become the plant.

The Non-Corporation moment

A new revolution begins with non- violence started by Mahatma Gandhi Ji in 1920. This revolution brings the new twist in the struggle of freedom for India. The Indian people not supported the Britisher's things and the movement went all over India. The moment ended in February 1922. These movements shook the roots of the British government.

1924 the last revolution

The revolution which almost brings freedom in India. The Quick India Moment was the revolution that gone through a lover India and the longest revolution in India in terms of the time period.

Freedom in India

Finally after the lots of struggle the nation got freedom. The conclusion from the struggle was finally built freedom.15 August 1947 India considered itself as the Independent state. The own constitution was written by the state.

CHAPTER TWO

ANCIENT PERSPECTIVE FOR INDEPENDENCE

There is no doubt that most history across the world has been written with a strong bias towards the victor and those in power. History of World War two is perhaps the best example where mainly British and Americans have been glorified and credited with achieving victory over Nazi Germany. Contribution of Russian and Indian war effort as partners of Allies has never been represented in its correct perspective. Western historians fail to concede that perhaps the turning point of second world war was the defeat of Nazi armies in Russia where they not only lost hundreds of thousands of soldiers but also a large part of their war machinery and equipment. Similarly, Nazi thrusts in Africa, Italy and along borders of France were mainly blunted by hundreds of thousands of Indian soldiers drafted in the British army. Same was the case in South East Asia against Japanese where Indian soldiers were sent to the front lines after British soldiers in Malay and other parts capitulated against Japanese onslaught.

By definition history is a continuous, systematic narrative of past events relating to a particular people, country, period, person, etc. It is written in a chronological order. It is important that history per se must be a true and factual record of events as they happened. This implies that history must record all the good, bad or ugly that may be associated with any period of time, event or personality. Opinions, perceptions or commentary on history and historical events should not be construed as history as they will vary from individual to individual.

Indian History can be divided in five broad periods – Vedic period from 6,500 BC to 1,000 BC, Golden period from 500 BC to 800 AD, Muslim period from 1,000 AD to 1,700 AD, British period from 1,700 AD to 1947 AD and finally the period after independence in 1947 which may be termed as contemporary History of India. The first two periods from 6,500 BC to 800 AD have a lot of gaps and the available history is rather sketchy. Without a doubt there is a need to fill the gaps and add more details where available. Most of this period relates to times when India and Indians were way ahead of most of the world in terms of development, civilization, arts and crafts, knowledge and civic administration. It is imperative for the nation to set the record straight. This will help to educate not only our own future generations but also rest of the world in highlighting and recording the contribution of India in various fields.

Muslim and British periods, as also contemporary history of India, are fairly well chronicled and documented. Muslim and British period history is written mainly from their perspective as most historians were commissioned by them. Therefore, Indian perspective is missing and hence the need for correction and addition of details where required. History related to Indian freedom struggle does appear to be loaded in favour of Congress. It is all about Nehru and Gandhi while contribution of others like Sardar Patel and a host of others has been minimized. Those who were part of the struggle but disagreed with Congress, like Subhash Chander Bose, appear to have been given a short shift or villainized. Lastly, contemporary history since 1947 is heavily biased with role and achievements of Congress party and its leaders being overstated while their follies have either been down played or omitted.

Today's history books describe Akbar as one of the greatest emperors of Mughal dynasty and he is referred to as 'Akbar the Great'. Will rewritten history continue to describe him as 'great'? How will Raja Man Singh, the brave and highly trusted Rajput commander of Akbar's armies, who helped Akbar to extend his empire in India be portrayed? Can he be forgiven for fighting with Maharana Pratap in the battle of Haldi Ghati on behalf of Akbar? In more recent times we have Subhash Chander Bose who raised an armed revolt against British much to the dislike of Gandhi, Nehru and Congress as a whole? Will he be the new champion of India's struggle for independence in place of Mahatma Gandhi? What about Lord Mountbatten whose dubious role during partition of India in 1947 leads to a lot of uncomfortable questions? Today, in hindsight, there are a lot of question marks on many decisions that were taken by Gandhi and Nehru, both during the struggle for independence and later in the initial years after independence. Will revised history vilify them for their mistakes? Will some of these historical figures lose their exalted status and be portrayed as villains instead?

What needs to be discussed is what should be added, what should be rewritten and what needs to be omitted from Indian history as it is available today. If one were to go by some political statements of leaders of BJP, it would appear that they wish to remove a lot of Mughal and British period History as it is not very flattering for Indian society. The state of Karnataka is already taking steps to delete Tippu Sultan from their History books. Indian history, as it stands today, describes him as a brave ruler who refused to bow to British and portrays him as a tolerant king in matters of religion. But today many assert that he was a bigot who converted thousands of Hindus to Islam forcibly and committed atrocities against them. How will the revised or rewritten history portray him? Will his fight against the British, as part of Indian freedom struggle, be forgotten in the quest to portray him as a bigot and an enemy of Hindus? Ideally history should record both aspects as long as they are factual instead of removing any reference to him from history books.

It is important to understand that history is about past and past cannot be undone. If that be so then it is logical to include all that happened during a period of time irrespective of whether it looks good or bad in today's context. History is not only about eulogizing past events or heroes. It is also about understanding why something that irks us today happened in that period. Today as Indians we may feel bad about why Mughals or British ruled us for centuries. But what is more important here is to understand why we were subjugated and what went wrong in our own Indian society that foreigners could lord over us, treat us like slaves and dirt for nearly one thousand years. We must be inquisitive about why Hindu rulers could never get together to fight the enemy? Why did we always have some in our midst who sided with the enemy to ensure defeat of their own? Why did such turn coats forget that the very enemy whom they were helping would finish them off too once their utility was over?

Thus, it is important for history to be recorded in an unbiased and objective manner. It must not pander to selfish interests of those in power or those who are charged with writing it. It will be foolish to delete events or periods that today we may be ashamed of or feel guilty about. Any move to delete parts of factual Mughal or British or contemporary history would be counterproductive. It is important for future generations to reflect and learn from mistakes made by their forefathers. What should be done is to complete our history by adding what is missing or rewriting what is factually incorrect. The valiant struggles of Guru Gobind Singh or Maharana Pratap during the Mughal period or those of Rani of Jhansi in 1857 against the British must be chronicled in all their glory and detail instead of giving them a passing reference. There are many missing links in History of India like the Ahom dynasty in Assam which ruled uninterrupted for nearly six centuries from 1,228 to 1826 AD but hardly finds any mention in history books. Same is the case with many kingdoms of Southern India like the Cholas and Pandya whose continuity for centuries or exploitation of foreign lands needs to be highlighted and understood.

No government, irrespective of which political party runs it, can be trusted to be objective and unbiased in writing history. Given the situation in our country today, any move to change anything in history as it stands today will give rise to a fierce, and mostly meaningless, political debate. The task therefore must be entrusted to an eminent panel that draws on best available minds in the country. It must not have any political representation. They must be tasked to chronicle history as it happened and how it happened with logical deductions. They must avoid adding any personal commentary, interpretations or perceptions. Let the later be reserved for the reader who reads it. History of our nation must convey one clear message to every Indian irrespective of his current caste, creed or religion. While India may have had the misfortune of being invaded by Mughals or British, they were not 'us' by any stretch of imagination. They came to loot our wealth and exploit our fragmented society. Their rule in India was an aberration in our history and a failure on part of our society to present a combined front. While these invaders and their rule over us is part of our history, they or their ways cannot be part of our heritage. Indian heritage is all about what was Indian, is Indian and our culture that has evolved over the centuries to represent our Indianness. Anything that is alien to India and Indian culture, may be part of our history, but cannot be part of our heritage.

CHAPTER THREE

Are We Free After 71 Years of Freedom?

It's now been 71 years of Independence. But even after seven decades of freedom, we are yet to experience it in a real sense. Free we are from the hold of British forces, but are we free from the clutches of poverty, unemployment, illiteracy?

This Independence Day, let's vow to get past the hurdles that still hold back India from achieving freedom in its truest sense.Freedom is an idea for which many have died — freedom from slavery, freedom from colonialism, freedom of speech, freedom of religion, freedom to protest, and many others which we often take for granted. On the eve of Independence Day, this issue is devoted to what freedom means for us.

On August 15, 1947, 330 million Indians, nearly 13 per cent of the world population at that time, were freed in one of the single-largest emancipations in human history. India formally began its tryst with destiny and, in two years, had located the beating heart of its Constitution in Article

19, which gave its citizens the freedom of speech and expression, to assemble peaceably and without arms, to form associations or unions, to move freely throughout our national territory and, with certain exceptions, to reside and settle in any part of the country. This Constitution-given right, the freedom of speech and expression, is what powers our pens as journalists and allows us to hold to account those in power and authority.

The 71st anniversary of our independence is a good time as any other to ask the question: How free are we? It also comes at a time when the state of many of these freedoms is being questioned. The Human Freedom Index (HFI), 2017, prepared by the Cato Institute, a Washington DC-based public policy research organisation, ranks India 102nd out of 159 countries. The HFI uses 79 indicators of personal and economic freedoms - from the rule of law to the freedom to trade internationally — to arrive at its results.Some satisfaction — we're better than China, which holds the 130th position, and we've moved up.

Cause for concern too — we have a long way to go before we reach the top quartile. The HFI also reveals an interesting correlation between freedom and prosperity. All the countries in the top quartile of freedom enjoy a significantly higher per capita income — $38,871 — than those in the least free quartile — $10,346. India's per capita income currently is $7,170, even more reason, I think, for the government to step up on its promise of delivering double-digit economic growth.

CHAPTER FOUR

CULTURE & HERITAGE

The Ministry of Culture plays a vital role in the preservation and promotion of art and culture. Its aim is to develop ways and means by which basic cultural and aesthetic values and perceptions remain active and dynamic among the people. It also undertakes programmes for the promotion of various manifestations of contemporary art. The Department is a nodal agency for commemorating significant events and celebrating centenaries of great artists.

Cultural heritage is the legacy of tangible and intangible heritage assets of a group or society that is inherited from past generations. Not all legacies of past generations are "heritage", rather heritage is a product of selection by society.

Cultural heritage includes tangible culture (such as buildings, monuments, landscapes, books, works of art, and artifacts), intangible culture (such as folklore, traditions, language, and knowledge), and natural heritage (including culturally significant landscapes, and biodiversity).[2] The term is often used in connection with issues relating to the protection of Indigenous intellectual property.

The deliberate act of keeping cultural heritage from the present for the future is known as preservation (American English) or conservation (British English), which cultural and historical ethnic museums and cultural centers promote, though these terms may have more specific or technical meanings in the same contexts in the other dialect. Preserved heritage has become an anchor of the global tourism industry, a major contributor economic value to local communities.

Legal protection of cultural property comprises a number of international agreements and national laws. United Nations, UNESCO and Blue Shield International deal with the protection of cultural heritage. This also applies to the integration of United Nations peacekeeping.

Lifestyle, Values & Beliefs

India is a diverse country, a fact that is visibly prominent in its people, culture and climate. From the eternal snows of the Himalayas to the cultivated peninsula of far South, from the deserts of the West to the humid deltas of the East, from the dry heat and cold of the Central Plateau to the cool forest foothills, Indian lifestyles clearly glorify the geography.

The food, clothing and habits of an Indian differ in accordance to the place of origin.

Culture

The Indian culture varies like its vast geography. People speak in different languages, dress differently, follow different religions, eat different food but are of the same temperament. So whether it is a joyous occasion or a moment of grief, people participate whole-heartedly, feeling the happiness or pain. A festival or a celebration is never constrained to a family or a home. The whole community or neighbourhood is involved in bringing liveliness to an occasion. Likewise, an Indian wedding is a celebration of union, not only of the bride and groom, but also of two families, maybe cultures or religion too! Similarly, in times of sorrow, neighbours and friends play an important part in easing out the grief.

CHAPTER FIVE

SCIENCE

The global image of India is that of an upcoming and progressive nation. True, India has leaped many boundaries in all sectors- commerce, technology and development etc in the recent past, yet she has not neglected her other creative genius. Wondering what it is? Well, it the alternative science that has been continuously practiced in India since times immemorial. Ayurveda, is a distinct form of medicine made purely of herbs and natural weeds, that can cure any ailment of the world. Ayurveda has also been mentioned in the Ancient Indian epics like Ramayana. Even today, when the western concept of medicine has reached its zenith, there are people looking for alternative methods of treatment for its multifarious qualities.

With increasing complexities in one's lives these days, people are perpetually looking for a medium through which they get some peace of mind. This is where another science, that of meditation and spirituality comes into the scene. Meditation and Yoga are synonymous with India and Indian spirituality. Meditation is one of the most important components of Yoga, which is a mind-body therapy involving a series of exercises. The word 'meditation' covers many disparate practices from visualizing situations, focusing on objects or images, thinking through a complex idea, or even getting lost in a provocative book, all qualifying as meditation in the broad sense. However in Yoga, meditation generally refers to the more formal practice of focusing the mind and observing oneself in the moment. Many people from India and abroad are resorting to yoga and meditation to de-stress and rejuvenate their mind.

Another widely followed phenomena in India is the Doctrine of Karma that preaches that every person should behave justly as every act or deed comes back in full circle in one of the births of an individual.

A very important aspect of India in the recent past is the emergence of the New Age woman. Women in India are predominantly homemakers, though this perspective is changing. In many places, especially metros and other cities, women are the bread earners of the house or are at par with their male counterparts. The increase in the cost of living/economy has also contributed to the rise in this aspect.

The beauty of the Indian people lies in their spirit of tolerance, give-and-take and a composition of cultures that can be compared to a garden of flowers of various colours and shades of which, while maintaining their own entity, lend harmony and beauty to the garden - India!

CHAPTER SIX

THE VALUE OF INDEPENDENCE

There are few virtues more important than independence. Independence is a requirement for leading your own life. How can you make decisions if every action you take has to be filtered through other people first? Without independence, you can't be the captain of your life. You must be satisfied scrubbing the decks while someone else sets the direction you're to follow.

Independence doesn't mean you never need other people. Most people wouldn't last a year stranded on an island with no other people to provide support. Independence means that you add at least as much value back as you take from every transaction. You don't leave a permanent debt between you and another person.

Debt is Dependency

When you build a debt with another person, you lose your independence. If you require another person to support you, that person has power over you. They can withdraw their funding based on your actions, effectively controlling your life. Even if they are benevolent, they may unconsciously use their power to influence your decisions.

If your transactions are fair, you retain your independence. I'm not dependent on a grocery store because, if they decide not to feed me, I can take my money elsewhere. Since it is an equal trade, there is no imbalance of power.

Independence is More Than Just Money

The debt that dependency creates doesn't just have to be in finances. You can be completely financially independent, but entirely socially and intellectually dependent on other people.

Financial independence is important. Requiring money from other people to live isn't ideal. Even if you are dependent on a spouse, family member or the government for an income, it shouldn't become a permanent situation.

If everyone became financially dependent on another person, the economy would collapse. Independence isn't just a personal virtue, it's a moral virtue. Avoiding debts with other people makes you in control over your own life. Independence also makes you a creator instead of a user. By putting back at least as much as they are taking, independent people ensure the world stays in balance.

Financial independence, and the consequences of financial dependence are easy to understand. It doesn't take a leap of thinking to realize that if everyone drains more money than they create, the world will collapse.

Social and intellectual independence are harder to see. But, I believe that they are even more important than financial independence. If you are financially dependent, another person has control over your body. They can decide whether you eat or starve. If you are socially or intellectually dependent, another person has control over your mind and soul.

Social Independence

Money isn't the only currency people use. Sure, it's the only kind you carry around in your wallet, but it is only one form of transactions. Social currency is another method of transactions. It is the currency of relationships, friendships, loyalty and service to other people.

Just as you can be financially dependent, you can be socially dependent. This means you are emotionally dependent on the opinions of the people around you. You care what other people think of you. Worse, you use their whims and biases as a foundation for making decisions on how to live your life.

Someone who is socially dependent can never be authentic. Instead they must constantly ask themselves whether what they are doing is popular or fashionable. I'm sure we both know people who fit this model. They are the people who care more about being liked than being themselves.

Independence here means the same thing it does with finances. It doesn't mean you don't need people and are happy living alone. It simply means that the relationship value you contribute outwards at least equals the value you take away. You aren't dependent on the opinions of other people because you can just as easily make new friends.

A person who has complete social independence feels free to leave friends and relationships that demand too high a price. Just as a financially independent woman wouldn't keep shopping at a store where the prices weren't worth the goods sold, a socially independent man wouldn't stick with friends who demanded that he become a fake in order to have their friendship.

Intellectual Independence

Intellectual independence is the most important form of independence. While it might not be easy, you can move from a position of social and financial dependence to one of independence. As long as you can make decisions for yourself, you can move closer towards complete independence.

Intellectual dependency is so damaging because, if you are dependent, it is incredibly difficult to break those chains. Intellectual dependency is the equivalent of selling your soul. While you can become a slave in body and in relationships, if you are a slave in the mind, you cease being a consciously deciding human being.

Intellectual dependence happens when you stop thinking for yourself. Instead of filtering ideas through your own powers of reasoning, you accept them blindly. You get caught onto dogma and superstition instead of what is true for you.

CHAPTER SEVEN

PLACES MAKE HISTORY

While we celebrate the Independence Day, we must remember that India did not get independence overnight. It was a struggle of almost 200 years! Our countrymen had to go through myriad difficulties to achieve the freedom and fighting someone so strong was not an easy task. The entire country played became a battle field and everyone contributed in every possible way. Let' have a look at those glorious places that played a crucial role India's independence struggle.

Barrackpore, West Bengal

As we all say "It started from here". The famous rebellion of 1857 started from Barrackpore, when a sepoy Mangal Pandey declared war against his commanders. It all actually started from here and we all still remember the bloodshed and war that happened after that. Even after so many years, the place still has memories from the grounds. For a true patriot, there are myriad places to visit here in the city.Places to visit in Barrackpore for a patriot: Mangal Pandey Park and Gandhi Museum.

Jhansi, Uttar Pradesh

The city of Jhansi, also known as the City of Rani Lakshmi Bai served as another place where the spark of Sepoy mutiny reached and later turned into war. Lakshmi Bai is one of the most famous and courageous female soldier crucial to Indian independence. She died on the battlefield fighting the British soldiers and got her name registered in history in golden words. Jhansi still remembers the contribution of this great warrior and bas dedicated several places to her.Places to visit in Jhansi for a patriot: Fort of Jhansi, Rani Mahal, Government Museum, Jhansi Museum and Gandhi Museum.

Bombay (now Mumbai), Maharashtra

Bombay was an important place during the Independence movement of India. Congress (now Indian National Congress) was founded in Bombay by Allan Octavian Hume. There are so many places in Mumbai that bear testimony to Indian freedom and make India proud with their existence!Places to visit in Mumbai for a patriot: Gateway of India.

Calcutta, (now Kolkata), Bengal

Calcutta remained the centre of Indian nationalism throughout the Indian Independence struggle. Indian National Association was the first nationalist organisation that was founded in Calcutta by Surendranath Banerjee and Anandamohan Bose. Calcutta was the hub of creative minds and Indian leaders and strategies were made here of how to free India from the chains of British.Places to visit in Calcutta for a patriot: Netaji Bhawan, Town Hall, Saheed Minar and Indian Museum.

Champaran, Bihar

Champaran Satyagraha was Mahatama Gandhi's first successful achievement after he came back from India. Britishers, at that time forced, Indian farmers to cultivate indigo, used for dying cloths and not the food crops that was necessary for survival. Gandhi fought non-violently and this later came to be the place from where non-violence politics started.Places to visit in Champaran for a patriot: Valmikinagar, Brindavan and Ashoka Pillars.

Jallianwala Bagh, Punjab

The Jallianwala Bagh is known for the Jallianwala Bagh massacre that took place on 13th April 1919. British Army Commander Reginald Dyer ordered his troops to open fire on the crowd of Baishakhi Pilgrims and non-violent protesters. Approximately 1650 rounds were fired on innocent crowd leading to 379 deaths and 1200 wounded (British government data). This was one of the cruellest acts of human slaughter in the history of Indian freedom struggle.Places to visit in Jallianwala Bagh for a patriot: Wagah Border.

Chauri Chaura, Uttar Pradesh

It is famous for the Chauri Chaura Incident, in which the police first killed several peaceful demonstrators and the angry mob in retaliation set the police chowki (Police Station) on fire, thereby killing 22 policemen. It was one of those incidents where people killed their own people.Places to visit in Chauri Chaura for a patriot: Shaheed Bandhu Singh Smarak.

CHAPTER EIGHT

Do We Deserve Our Freedom

This Independence Day let us question how we are fulfilling our responsibilities to the nation as we enjoy our Freedom!

Seventy-one years after India gained freedom, we need to take this celebration to the next level. After all, a vast majority of Indians today has only ever known a free India. We have been born to the freedom that our forefathers fought and died for.

Do we stop to think of the sacrifices made, and what it meant to be treated as second-class citizens in our own country? Or is that just relegated to our history books and then left behind along with our years as students? Do we make an attempt to carry that baton, or does it lie unattended?

What then gives us the right to enjoy and celebrate a freedom that we are doing nothing to salvage and nourish? Can we say that we have done our best to ensure that the sacrifices of our Freedom Fighters were not in vain? Are we conscious of our duty to them or to our country? It is time now that we too contribute towards a Freedom we enjoy mindlessly.

We can no longer cover our ears when we hear the screams of orphans from Muzaffarpur's Balika Grih shelter home; we must step out to rescue the children. We cannot put on blinkers so as not to confront unfair practices; we cannot throw around litter or work against the environment with impunity. We must not pay up corrupt officials rather than make a complaint and fight it out. Why are we scared to be involved, of harm coming to us? Have you wondered what would have happened if that had been the attitude of our Freedom Fighters?

We complain, we curse our country and circumstances, but we cannot be cynical and hopeless if we wish for a better future. We have to believe. And we have to let that belief fuel our ambitions and our everyday life. Our Freedom has to have the backing of values and a vision for the future else it is nothing but a wild, untamed beast leading us nowhere. Just as we have personal goals and a vision for our kids and our future, we must have similar goals and vision for our nation as well.

No freedom can be enjoyed unless we also shoulder the responsibility that comes with it. So we need to shape up and do our bit. Right from the most powerful industrialist in the country to the safai karamchari working on the streets – everyone has a job and a responsibility towards the nation – we must all ask ourselves how we are fulfilling that?

We all need to work towards a larger purpose – towards the universal spirit of Being Indian – to be proud of our country, understand her strengths and work on her weaknesses – so that we can all stand proud and happy when we actually walk into India Shining or Achche Dinn!

To begin with, let us start small – with ourselves, our homes, neighbourhoods and the people, animals and environment around us. How can that be made better with the available resources? Let us gather ideas, debate, raise our voices and be part of the dialogues that are so sorely needed.

Let us look for avenues that give us an opportunity to participate in nation building. Let us insist the government provides us such venues and platforms from where we can hold peaceful and amicable dialogues for bettering the future – a responsibility that is as much ours as it is the government's.

Let us rid ourselves of the fear that pervades the country right now – a fear that stops us from speaking up, tweeting, commenting – or shouting in protest. Let us join the voices that still speak, that know no fear, that raise questions and seek answers. Let us also contribute to the strategic dialogues so needed to take us ahead.

No, you are not too small a cog in the wheel to make a difference; don't give up even before you begin! Every single one of us matters. Let us learn from our past and use it to boost our present and fuel our future.

CHAPTER NINE

CONCLUSION

Freedom the part of everyone's life. The life of an Independent is not only freedom. From our childhood, we want freedom we want to walk ourselves, want to speak our own words and even as we grow our freedom rise, it's demand we want our own rules in our life. Freedom for life has a different meaning but when it comes to the nation than it becomes everything. Freedom of the nation means to create a nation that gives the right to do everything freely in the nation. There are many nations who fought for their freedom, India one of the nation that creates history in struggling for freedom.

India a vast country and has a huge army but then also it has been ruled by different persons and nations. People have to fight for their freedom. The legal rights were not given to the people of the nation. The British ruled India for nearly 200 years and exploited the peoples of India although having numerous army At that time, the question arose, how to start for the independence of the country. India was not able to get the freedom until the peoples get united and fought in an organization. There are numerous organization and army troops formed let's read about these in brief and also check the conclusion of the Indian freedom struggle.

British in India

British has started to conquer India during the Battle of Plassey in 1757. The Beitishehsr's achieve political power in India. The establishment of political power and the company was during the time period of lord governor Dalhousie. During the tenure of Lord Dalhousie, the company almost started to rule entire India. In 1948 Lord Dalhousie Became the governor-general of India. This was the best time of the British in India.

First Revolution of India

The very first revolution for freedom was started in 1847. The revolution was started but the unity causes and becomes the failure of the struggle. The main lead was done by the Rani Laxmi Bai the queen of Jhansi. This can be the victory for the nation but the conclusion of the struggle for the nation was only the start. The seed of freedom and feeling of nationalism was uprooted in India.

Revolt of 1857

After the end of the time period of the governor Lord Dalhousie. The Indians again formed a new revolution this revolution was almost all around the nation. The new thing about this revolution is it was started by the solider's who are in the army of British. The Hindu and Muslim both were equally joined the revolution in the nation. This there was unity but the timing of the revolution was not perfect which causes failure. Thus the struggle for freedom was not over the seed of freedom has become the plant.

The Non-Corporation moment

A new revolution begins with non- violence started by Mahatma Gandhi Ji in 1920. This revolution brings the new twist in the struggle of freedom for India. The Indian people not supported the Britisher's things and the movement went all over India. The moment ended in February 1922. These movements shook the roots of the British government.

1924 the last revolution

The revolution which almost brings freedom in India. The Quick India Moment was the revolution that gone through a lover India and the longest revolution in India in terms of the time period.

Freedom in India

Finally after the lots of struggle the nation got freedom. The conclusion from the struggle was finally built freedom.15 August 1947 India considered itself as the Independent state. The own constitution was written by the state.

9 798886 064483

Printed by Libri Plureos GmbH in Hamburg, Germany